MY BIBLE STORY LIBRARY

JOSEPH
AND THE
COAT OF
MANY COLORS

LANDOLL'S®

Landoll, Inc.
Ashland, Ohio 44805
© Oyster Books Ltd. 1992

Jacob was a wealthy old shepherd who lived in Canaan with his twelve sons. Jacob loved all his sons, but his favorite was Joseph.

One day Jacob gave Joseph a wonderful coat. It had long sleeves and, unlike his brothers' plain coats, it had lots of brightly-colored stripes and patterns. Joseph's brothers were jealous.

"We work harder than Joseph," they grumbled to each other as they watched the flocks of sheep, "but he always gets special treatment. And now he's been given that coat of many colors. It's just not fair."

But Joseph was not very nice to his brothers, either. Sometimes he went with them to help look after the sheep.

When he came home, he ran and told his father everything his brothers had said and done during the day.

This made matters worse. Joseph's brothers could hardly bear to talk to him. They refused to allow him to come and look after the sheep any more. So Joseph stayed at home.

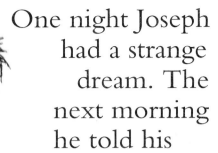

One night Joseph had a strange dream. The next morning he told his brothers all about it.

"I dreamt that we were all in the fields tying up sheaves of wheat," he explained. "When we finished, my sheaf stood up straight and all your sheaves stood in a circle around mine and bowed down to it."

"And do you suppose that means we will all bow down to you one day?" snorted Joseph's brothers, angrily. "You must be crazy!"

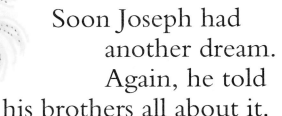

Soon Joseph had another dream. Again, he told his brothers all about it.

"This time," he said. "I saw the sun, the moon and eleven stars bowing down to me."

The brothers were speechless with rage. Even Jacob was upset.

"Are you trying to tell us that the whole family should bow down to you?" he asked angrily.

"Well, I've heard quite enough. I don't want to know any more about these dreams of yours."

The dreams made Joseph's brothers hate Joseph even more. But Jacob began to wonder if God was trying to tell him that Joseph had been chosen to be special in some way.

A few days later, Joseph's brothers drove their flocks into the hills, looking for fresh grass for the sheep to eat. They were away for many days, and Jacob grew worried. He decided to send Joseph to look for them.

"Go and find your brothers," Jacob told Joseph. "Take them some food and make sure that they are well and happy."

It took Joseph a long time to find his brothers, but at last he saw their camp in the distance.

Joseph's brothers recognized him immediately. He was wearing his brightly-colored coat.

"Look," they said to each other. "Here comes the Dreamer. Let's teach him a lesson he'll never forget."

Some of the brothers wanted to kill Joseph. But Reuben, the eldest, thought this was too cruel.

"We can't kill our own brother," he protested. "Let's just throw him into that dried-up well over there, without hurting him."

The brothers decided that Reuben's plan was best, so when Joseph walked into the camp they grabbed him. They tore off his coat of many colors and threw him roughly into the well.

Reuben, glad that his brother was still alive, walked away to tend to the sheep. He secretly hoped he might be able to rescue Joseph later and take him home.

The other brothers sat down to enjoy the food which Joseph had brought. While they were eating, they saw a long line of camels coming toward them.

They soon realized that the men with the camels were traders, on

their way to Egypt to sell spices and other goods.

"Why don't we sell Joseph to the traders?" suggested Judah, one of the brothers. "They will take him to Egypt, sell him as a slave, and he'll never bother us again."

The others thought this was a brilliant idea. They shouted to the traders to stop. Then they hauled Joseph out of the well.

Although Joseph was dirty, the traders could see that he was young, healthy and strong.

"What will you pay us for this young man?" asked the brothers. "He will fetch a good price in Egypt, as a slave."

"Twenty silver pieces," came the reply.

"Agreed!" shouted the brothers.

The traders counted out the twenty pieces of silver, and led Joseph away.

As soon as they reached home, the brothers went to Jacob. They pretended to be very sad.

"We found Joseph's coat," they told their father. "He must have been killed by a wild animal."

Jacob was completely taken in by their trick. He burst into tears, thinking that his favorite son was dead. He did not notice the sly looks his sons gave each other.

But Jacob need not have worried. His favorite son was quite safe. In fact, Jacob had been right all along. God did have a plan for Joseph, and part of that plan was going to Egypt. There Joseph would learn many important things.

And one day, the whole family would meet again and be friends. But that is another story.